SOFTBALL: FIELD & EQUIPMENT

BARBARA BONNEY

The Rourke Corporation, Inc.
Vero Beach, Florida 32964

Barbara Bonney is a librarian and freelance writer in Cincinnati, Ohio. Besides enjoying research and words, she likes creating with food and fabrics. She has two children.

PHOTO CREDITS:
© Tony Gray: cover, pages 7, 9, 10, 12, 15, 16, 18, 21, 22; © East Coast Studios: page 6, 13, 19; © the National Softball Hall of Fame and Museum, Oklahoma City, OK: page 4

EDITORIAL SERVICES:
Susan Albury

Library of Congress Cataloging-in-Publication Data

Bonney, Barbara, 1955-
   Softball, field and equipment / by Barbara Bonney.
     p. cm. — (Softball)
   Includes index
   Summary: Discusses two essential elements of the game of softball: the field on which the game is played and the equipment used in the game.
   ISBN 0-86593-480-0
   1. Softball fields—Juvenile literature. 2. Softball—Equipment and supplies—Juvenile literature. [1. Softball fields. 2. Softball—Equipment and supplies. 3. Softball.]
I. Title. II. Series: Bonney, Barbara, 1955- Softball.
GV881.15.B64 1998
796.357'06—dc21
                                98–11087
                                  CIP
                                  AC

Printed in the USA

TABLE OF CONTENTS

HISTORY

Softball was first played in 1887. Someone tied an old boxing glove into a ball and threw it at a man who had a broomstick. The large soft ball didn't travel far so they could play indoors. The game grew and teams played all winter. The sport went outdoors in the spring and went by many names: Kitten Ball, Mush Ball, Indoor-Outdoor, Playground Ball, and others. In 1926 it was named softball and in 1933 a group met to decide the rules.

Today this **Amateur** (AM a tur) Softball Association and other groups such as National Softball Association and Independent Softball Association decide the rules for the teams that they oversee.

In the 1887 softball rules, masks and gloves were not necessary but knee pads were recommended.

Long pants were common for women in the 1930s and 1940s.

THE FIELD

A softball field's size depends on who is playing. The bases are 55 feet (16.77 meters) apart for players under age ten with a pitching distance of 35 feet (10.76 meters) and a fence 150 feet (45.73 meters) from home plate.

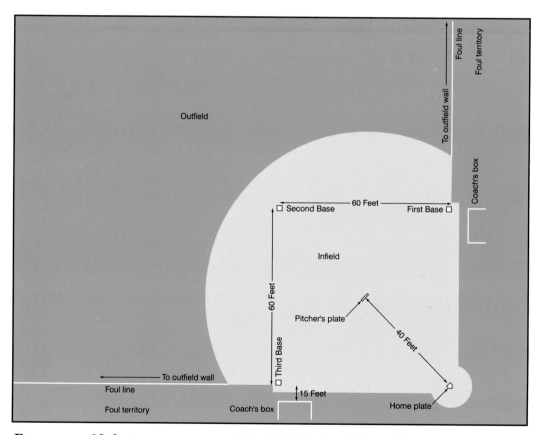

Bases are 60 feet apart on a softball field sized for older teens.

A softball field has both grass and dirt areas.

The field gets a little larger as the players get older. By age 15-18, the bases are 60 feet (18.29 meters) apart, pitching distance is 40 feet (12.19 meters), and the fence is 200 feet (60.97 meters) from home plate. Adults play on fields that are at least 265 feet (80.77 meters). Everything on the playing field has a proper measurement, even the bases.

BATS

From a distance, softball bats may look alike except for color. All bats have three parts: the knob, the reach, and the barrel. Reaches are often wrapped with tape to give a better gripping surface. Looking closer, you can see small differences. They could be made of **graphite** (GRA fite) or of white ash wood, but most are **aluminum alloy** (uh LOO muh num AL loy).

Also, some bats are thin but ones used in fast-pitch have a bottle shape. This larger barrel makes hitting the ball easier. Bats have different lengths for different-sized players. Bats should not be left unprotected from the weather and should be checked for safety. A baseball bat may not be used in softball.

Softball bats have different lengths and slightly different shapes.

BALLS

Softballs differ in hardness, the "core factor" of the ball. A higher core factor means a harder ball. The centers are made of **kapok** (KAY pok) or a mix of cork and rubber. Balls are usually 12 inches (30.48 centimeters) around and weigh 6 ounces (170.25 grams). The cover must be leather. Rubber covers wear longer but are not used in games. Most softball covers are stitched on so that the stitching shows, like a baseball.

Softballs with softer rubber covers, fleece balls or other soft softballs are fine for indoor use. They cannot be hit as far and are great to use when space is a problem.

A new women's professional softball league, Women's Professional Fastpitch (WPF) began in North Carolina on May 30, 1997.

The large size of a softball makes it easier to catch than a baseball.

GLOVES AND MITTS

Gloves and mitts protect hands and help players catch the ball. Gloves have three or four fingers and a thumb connected by a webbed pocket that holds the ball. Mitts look more like mittens, with a thumb and large area for all four fingers together. Mitts also have a webbed pocket.

This glove is being broken in to make it more flexible.

Mitts can be used by first base players and catchers who need the extra padding to protect the hand.

Only catchers and first base players have a choice to use a mitt instead of a glove in a game.

A softball glove's fingers are much longer than a hand, which helps in catching. A glove should be comfortable on the nonthrowing hand and the wearer should be able to control it. Players often stick a finger out the back of the glove for better control in catching the ball.

SHOES

Beginning players do not have to wear special shoes. Any type of sneaker that supports the foot in motion is fine. When skills improve, softball shoes made of leather canvas, vinyl or nylon can be worn. Adults are allowed to wear **spikes** (SPYKS) in some situations but kids cannot wear spikes at all. The chance of injury is high for the wearer and other players. Rubber **cleats** (KLEETS) help in running and turning quickly but do not injure players like spikes do.

To smooth out a cormer when base running, run a little outside of the baseline, then angle to the base and touch its inside tip.

Cleats on the bottom of shoes help the player's feet grip the field.

BASES

In practice or playing just for fun, bases can be anything. But in a game, they must be a certain size. Home plate and the pitcher's plate are usually made of rubber. Home plate is five-sided, with the front edge measuring 17 inches (43.18 centimeters). Pitcher's plate is 24 inches (60.96 centimeters) long. The other bases are usually made of canvas and are 15 inches (38.1 centimeters) square and not more than 5 inches (12.7 centimeters) thick.

Sometimes kids' games have a double base—an orange base and a white base side by side. The runner touches the orange half and the baseman touches the white half. This prevents players from **colliding** (koh LYD ing) and getting injured.

An orange-and-white double base keeps players from running into each other.

UNIFORMS AND EQUIPMENT

The uniform worn by a team must be the same color and style for each player. The style can be like a baseball uniform which can cost a lot of money, or just shorts and T-shirts that look alike. If players will be sliding, pants and padding will protect them from scrapes.

A uniform with long pants will protect legs in a slide. Ball caps with bills shield the eyes from the sun.

This base runner wears a helmet as protection from a moving ball.

Catchers might not wear protective padding in a slow-pitch game, but always wear it in fast-pitch. Helmets protect batters, runners, and on-deck batters from head injury when playing close to the ball, though not all softball players wear them.

Score books are necessary at a game and rule books and a measuring tape are handy. Teams often have their own bats, balls, **rosin** (ROZ in) bags, batting helmets, and bases. Younger teams may have tees to bat from.

TEAMS

Any group of nine or ten players can be a team. Players who want to improve with regular practice, drills, and coaching should join a team connected with an organization that has league rules. Teams learn these rules from their coaches.

A coach, using a positive attitude and lots of practice, teaches respect for players, other coaches, and umpires. The best coaches know players need conditioning and not just skills, and each player has strengths and weaknesses. The coach tries to help each player improve and then puts each one in a position that will make the team perform at its best.

Beginning softball players might use "Incrediballs" or Reduced Injury Factor balls that are softer than official softballs.

In a team meeting, the coach gives players tips and encouragement.

GLOSSARY

aluminum alloy (uh LOO muh num AL loy) — material made of aluminum mixed with another metal to make it stronger

amateur (AM a tur) — someone who plays a game for fun and not money

cleats (KLEETS) — wedge-shaped pieces of metal or rubber on the bottom of sport shoes to help gripping

colliding (koh LYD ing) — running into something

graphite (GRA fite) — a type of carbon that is mixed with other materials to make them stronger

kapok (KAY pok) — a light cottony fiber from the seed pods of the silk-cotton tree

rosin (ROZ in) — a product made from tree sap which helps hands get sticky

spikes (SPYKS) — the sharp points on the bottom of a sport shoe, used for gripping

The equipment a player wears depends on the position being played.

INDEX

FURTHER READING

Find out more about softball with these helpful books and information sites:
Elliott, Jill & Martha Ewing, eds. *Youth Softball: A Complete Handbook.* printed by Brown & Benchmark, 1992
Rookie Coaches Softball Guide/American Sport Education Program. Human Kinetics Publishers, Inc., 1992
Cohen, Neil, ed. *The Everything You Wanted to Know About Sports Encyclopedia.* Bantam Books, 1994
Boehm, David A., editor-in-chief. *Guinness Sports Record Book 1990-91.* Sterling Publishing Co., Inc. 1990

on the internet at
www.softball.com/othrlink.htm (links to organizations, equipment manufacturers, teams, etc)